PETER HARRI.

ARCHAEOLOGY OF THE ENGLISH CIVIL WAR

SHIRE ARCHAEOLOGY

Cover photograph
Donnington Castle, Berkshire.
The gatehouse of the medieval castle is all that remains
standing after the Civil War sieges.
(Photograph: Cadbury Lamb.)

British Library Cataloguing in Publication Data:
Harrington, Peter.
Archaeology of the English Civil War. —
(Shire Archaeology Series; No. 68).
I. Title. II. Series.
941.06.
ISBN 0-7478-0156-8.

Published by
SHIRE PUBLICATIONS LTD
Cromwell House, Church Street, Princes Risborough,
Buckinghamshire HP27 9AJ, UK.

Series Editor: James Dyer

ISBN 0 7478 0156 8.

First published 1992.

Printed in Great Britain by
C. I. Thomas & Sons (Haverfordwest) Ltd,
Press Buildings, Merlins Bridge, Haverfordwest, Dyfed SA61 1XF.

Contents

Acknowledgements

I would like to acknowledge the assistance of several people who have provided information over the years on Civil War sites, particularly Mr Christopher Taylor and the late Mr R. A. Curphey. The following have provided information on newly excavated sites: Mr Malcolm Atkin, Mr Alan Turton, Mr Terrence A. James, Mr David Evans and Mr Martin Papworth. Others who have provided assistance with this study or answered enquiries include Dr L. S. Garrard, Mr Alex James, Mr Carl Crossan, Mrs P. J. Mansergh, Ms Anne Waite, Ms Carole Ryan, Ms R. H. Nossek, Mr H. V. Radcliffe, Mr Andrew Robertshaw, Mr Nicholas Johnson, Mr Simon Ward, Mr Michael Osborne, Mr Denis Peel, Mr M. E. Farley and Mr Eric Houlder. Dr Peter Newman provided details of the survey work at Marston Moor. I would like to give particular thanks to Mr John R. Kenyon of the National Museum of Wales, who offered advice and kindly read through the text, and to Mrs Stephanie Taylor and Mr Christopher Taylor, who have been of invaluable assistance in the preparation of the text for publication.

List of illustrations

1
Introduction

The Civil War which was fought across England, Scotland and Wales intermittently for almost a decade from 1642 until 1651, and in Ireland in 1649, was the first 'modern' war fought in the British Isles. More importantly, it was the first internal conflict that reflected the prevalence of gunpowder in all its forms. There were pitched battles but it was siege warfare which dominated the conflict as the belligerents struggled to gain control of major communication points, ports and regional centres. No town or castle was safe and every strongpoint was a target.

This is reflected in the archaeology of the period, where the emphasis has been on fortifications, whether they are remains of a fortified enceinte around a town, a battery overlooking a castle or a fort commanding a major line of communication. Many of these sites, particularly those away from urban centres, have left distinctive traces on the ground, although there is increasing evidence for town defences and the complex forms of fortification used to protect urban populations against the enemy.

Throughout the fifteenth and sixteenth centuries warfare had been revolutionised by the use of gunpowder and by the substantial progress in the effectiveness and destructive powers of artillery. As a result changes in forms and methods of defence were rapid.

These changes are still visible today in the obvious differences between the small stone coastal forts built by Henry VIII in the 1540s and the great defence works erected a few years later by Elizabeth I. The former usually have small circular or semicircular keeps with attached rounded gun platforms or batteries, as at the 'castles' of Deal and Walmer in Kent, Calshot and Hurst in Hampshire and St Mawes, Cornwall. The latter were often large defended areas with complex bastions, ditches and outworks. The defences at Berwick-upon-Tweed, Northumberland (1558-70), are the best examples of this although smaller instances still remain, as at Carisbrooke Castle on the Isle of Wight (1585-97). Both types of defences can be seen at Pendennis Castle, Cornwall (1540 and 1598).

The earthwork defences of the Civil War should represent the continuing development of military thinking and indeed some certainly do. The influence of new continental methods of fortification, particularly French and Dutch developments, are apparent at several surviving sites such as those around Newark, Nottinghamshire, and in contemporary plans of defence works such as that of Oxford. The form of bastion especially indicates advances in thought as to the most effective way of repelling attacks.

However, the very nature of the Civil War, and in particular the backgrounds and abilities of its combatants and their leaders, gives the physical remains of that conflict a special interest and demands a more careful approach to the understanding of their construction. For the defences of the English Civil War were produced by a curious dichotomy between military expertise and ignorance.

On the one hand there were soldiers and military engineers, both English and foreign, who had up-to-date knowledge and experience of contemporary warfare on the continent and who were used by both sides to considerable advantage. Thus Bernard de Gomme, who was later to be Charles II's chief engineer and was to build many late seventeenth-century fortresses for his master, designed and built the Royalist defences at Oxford. Similarly the variety of siegeworks erected around Colchester, Essex, for the siege of 1648 by Sir Thomas Fairfax suggests that the designer had considerable experience of continental warfare (figure 1).

On the other hand, military talent and experience were very limited in England in the mid seventeenth century. The last real war involving large numbers of English troops had been in Ireland in Elizabeth I's reign. There was not, nor had there ever been, a standing army and most of the troops fighting on either side in the Civil War were ill trained. There was considerable ideological commitment and no lack of volunteers at least in the early stages of the war, and towards its end the New Model Army was a relatively well organised group of regiments, but both sides always lacked experienced officers. Even where professionals who had served in the Dutch, Swedish or Spanish armies were available, politics affected their use. For the Royalists at least, because many of these professionals were Roman Catholics they could not be employed overtly without playing into the hands of enemy propagandists. As has been rightly said, 'it was for the most part a very amateur war' (Woolrych, 1961, 38).

As a result defence works were often extremely primitive or non-existent. At small centres in particular, the garrison often merely created simple banks and ditches, or in several instances merely put chains across a road as obstacles to disrupt the movement of the enemy. In such cases it is often difficult to determine whether some simple earthworks do represent remains from the war. Even when they can be so identified, the standard of construction seems to have left much to be desired. The tiny fort or 'sconce' at March in Cambridgeshire has indeed two bastions, albeit badly laid out, but there are no ramparts and its overall size makes it indefensible.

Further evidence of the rebellion can be seen at many castles, churches and cathedrals, in the form of mutilated carvings or graffiti, demolished (slighted) or battered masonry, bullet holes in doors and walls, or the marks made by cannonballs upon town or castle walls. The battlefields themselves show little surface evidence of the war although artefacts have been recovered from several sites. Few modern surveys have been undertaken on Civil War battlefields.

In any discussion of the field evidence and other material remains of war it is important to bear in mind that not only are the normal rules of life suspended but also that the organisation of warfare itself is frequently far removed from its theoretical ideal. Standardisation falls short and improvisation of weapons and equipment occurs. Besieged garrisons resort to extreme means of defending themselves when their regular supplies of food, ammunition and weaponry fail. Victims of war are hastily buried where they died. Uncertainty leads to an increase in the hiding of valuables and in the number of coin hoards, and domestic buildings are likely to be demolished to make way for fortifications or to clear fields of fire. These factors are common to most wars but in the case of the English Civil War are further emphasised by the short period of time — less than a decade — to which the material remains relate. It is therefore possible to establish with some degree of accuracy when particular objects were used.

Classification of sites

The following brief comments serve as an introduction to the types of sites and field monuments relating to the Civil War. Each type of site will be discussed in a separate chapter.

Castles and fortified houses. While the function of the castle was in decline by the mid seventeenth century this did not stop the opposing forces from garrisoning and refortifying numerous medieval strongholds. Indeed, many castles and fortified houses experienced bitter sieges, frequently over prolonged periods, thus demonstrating that such structures still provided formidable obstacles to an advancing force armed with artillery. Evidence of refortification exists at a number of sites while excavations have revealed occupation sequences dating from the war. These sites are described in detail in chapter 3.

Town defences. Virtually every major town and city in England underwent some form of defensive fortification as a result of the war, however crude and temporary it might have been. Elsewhere earlier defences were adapted. In a few instances traces of Civil War defences survive above ground, although the majority were destroyed by

1. Plan of the siege of Colchester, Essex, by Parliamentary forces in 1648, from a broadsheet published by W. Keymer and including a diary of the siege. (Reproduced by courtesy of the Trustees of the British Museum.)

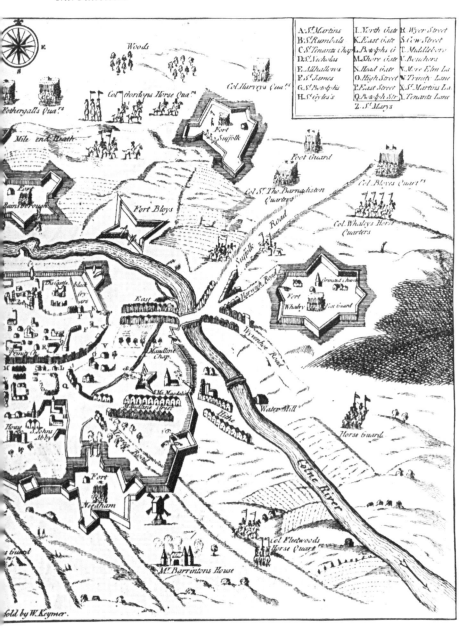

A. St Martins
B. St Rumbals
C. St Tenants Chap.
D. St Nicholas
E. Allhallows
F. St James
G. St Botolphs
H. St Gyles's

I. North Gate
K. East Gate
L. Botolphs G.
M. Shore Gate
N. Head Gate
O. High Street
P. East Street
Q. Botolph Str.
Z. St Marys

R. Wyer Street
S. Cow Street
T. Middleboro
V. Bouchers
W. More Elm La
X. Trinity Lane
Y. St Martins La.
Z. Tenants Lane

nineteenth- and twentieth-century urban development. At several centres intensive archaeological work has produced evidence of these fortifications and further work will undoubtedly reveal more. Town defences are discussed fully in chapter 4.

Siegeworks and forts. While few siegeworks have survived, of all the sites dating from the war independent forts are the most prominent field monuments. Because they are mostly situated in rural areas a greater number have survived. The largest concentration of both forts and siegeworks can be seen around Newark-on-Trent in Nottinghamshire (RCHM, 1964) although other forts exist, particularly in Cambridgeshire. These sites form the subject of chapter 5.

Other sites and evidence. Many islands and coastal areas provided important havens for naval vessels during the war and their defence was vital, particularly for the Royalists, who depended upon supplies from the continent. Small batteries and other fortifications have survived in these areas. Elsewhere prehistoric, Roman and medieval sites were adapted for use during the war or served as siegeworks. Artefacts turn up occasionally on battlefields; however, the only major survey has been on Marston Moor. The numismatics of the period, based on evidence from coin hoards and siege money, is gradually being understood. These sites are described in chapter 6.

2
Early work on Civil War sites

In the years immediately following the Restoration in 1660 the remains of the war were looked upon with curiosity by some while others urged their demolition to erase the visible scars of the conflict. Yet others, who were concerned with the art of siege warfare, used them as examples of fortification in their various treatises. Philip Staynred included a plan of the remains of the Royal Fort, Bristol, to demonstrate the design of an irregular fort in his 'Compendium of Fortification' published in *The Mariner's Magazine* of 1678. The surveyor Captain James Archer of the Royal Engineers used a plan of the Royalist sconce at York known as The Mount in his map of that city drawn in 1682. In 1725 William Stukeley visited the same site and described it as 'a great sconce a little way off York called The Mount, consisting of four bastions raised in the civil wars' (RCHM, *York*, 1972). In the same year Daniel Defoe recorded the existence of the Civil War fortifications at York, although he noted that many were then being demolished. The description by a York historian of the levelling of The Mount in 1742 mentions the discovery, among other things, of two cannon bullets, a crossbow shot and some musket balls.

Francis Grose noted several sites in his book *The Antiquities of England and Wales*, published between 1783 and 1797. One example he gave was Beeston Castle, Cheshire: 'Many traces of these operations (the siege of 1645), such as ditches, trenches, and other military works, are still discernible in the grounds about it'. His description of Donnington Castle, Berkshire, and the Civil War defences 'amongst the bushes and briars with which they are at present overgrown', was accompanied by a plan showing the remains (figure 2). The surviving defences built around Raglan Castle in Gwent were represented on a plan in W. Coxe's *An Historical Tour in Monmouthshire* published in 1801, while the possible Civil War fort at Penrhos Farm, north-east of Caerleon, Gwent, was described by Coxe as being perhaps the remains of a Roman camp which had been altered and strengthened during the war. Later antiquarians referred to sites of Civil War fortifications but often failed to recognise them as such. A possible battery of the period at Market Lavington, Wiltshire, was described by Colt Hoare in 1812 as 'the mutilated banks of a square earthen work'.

Occasionally early mapmakers included Civil War fortifications in their town plans, and illustrations of these sites sometimes appeared in eighteenth- and nineteenth-century engravings. An example is the fort on Paddington Green, London, which no longer exists but which appears as a shapeless mound in a Victorian engraving. In the nineteenth century there was a resurgence of interest in the war inspired by the writings of Macaulay and Scott, coupled with a growth in antiquarianism. Some sites and battlefields of the war were 'examined' during this

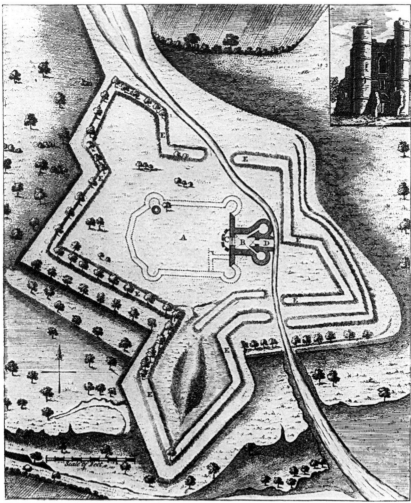

2. Plan of Donnington Castle, Berkshire, and its outworks, from Grose's *Antiquities* (1783-97). Grose's key reads: A, the castle in ruins; B, the entrance with the towers standing; C, a drinking room erected by the proprietor; D, another porch open at top; E, temporary works thrown up in the Civil Wars; between the vaulted passage B and drinking room C, the steps is [*sic*] a vacancy for a port cullis.

period. Among these was Lamel Hill at York, which was excavated by Dr John Thurnam in 1849. One of the earliest workers to write on the subject of Civil War defences was Lieutenant Colonel William E. Ross of the Royal Engineers, who discussed the military engineering of the war and included plans of a number of towns (Ross, 1887). He stated that, while there was no native school of military architecture in Britain at the time, many of the fortifications were built by foreign engineers using continental principles. These, however, were no more than provisional or semi-permanent structures and were often purely additions to existing walls. While Ross was the first to consider the whole question of the fortifications of the 1640s, he failed to mention surviving sites. It was not until the publication of A. Hadrian Allcroft's *Earthwork of England* in 1908 that the question of existing sites was raised. In chapter 17 of the book, the author discussed the monuments and included those at Newark-on-Trent (Nottinghamshire), Earith (Cambridgeshire), Cambridge Castle, and Basing House (Hampshire), as well as reused earlier sites. Plans of some of these sites were also included. Allcroft did alert the reader to the problem of dating many fortifications such as those found around country mansions and castles; these often bore no relation to the events of the Civil War or were simply reused from earlier periods. In the same year that Allcroft's book appeared a small excavation was carried out on the Bulwark at Earith (see chapter 5).

The great scholar of castles and fortifications Bryan St John O'Neil took Allcroft's work further by examining particular sites in detail. In 1936 he discussed the Civil War forts of Gallant's Bower and Mount Ridley at Dartmouth, Devon, and, in another paper two years later, the surviving works at Carmarthen, Dyfed. The battery at Cornbury Park, Oxfordshire, was the subject of a 1945 paper, and in his *Castles and Cannon* of 1960 he noted over thirty survivals from the war. He documented the works on the Scilly Isles in 1961.

The first and only detailed examination of Civil War sites appeared in 1964. In that year the Royal Commission on Historical Monuments published *Newark on Trent: the Civil War Siegeworks*, which recorded over a dozen earthworks surviving around that town. Since then there have been a few major studies, particularly on town defences discovered during excavations, as at Chester, Exeter and Gloucester. Work at a number of castles, among them Sandal Castle, West Yorkshire (Mayes and Butler, 1983), has produced considerable evidence of the war. Archaeological work has been undertaken at several Civil War sites including Caerphilly (Mid Glamorgan), Maumbury Rings (Dorchester, Dorset) and Burnswark (Dumfries and Galloway). Plans and a gazetteer of surviving sites appeared in 1987 (Harrington, 1987; figure 3).

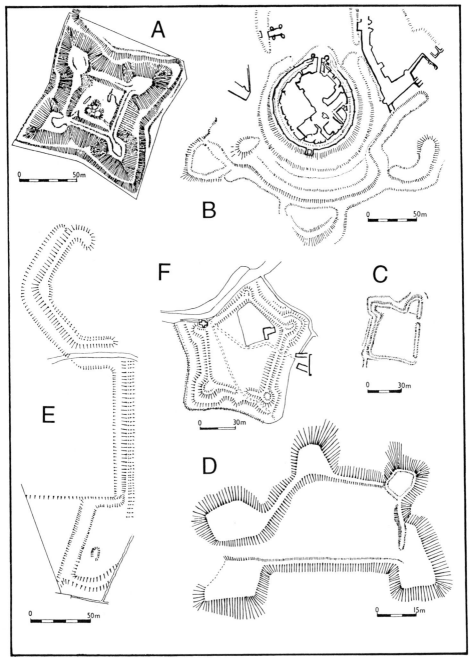

3. Plans of surviving Civil War sites. A, The Queen's Sconce, Newark, Nottinghamshire. B, Basing House, Hampshire. C, Stoke Lodge, Newark. D, Gallant's Bower, Dartmouth, Devon. E, Carmarthen, Dyfed. F, Horsey Hill, Cambridgeshire. (After Harrington, 1987.)

3
Castles and fortified houses

Many castles and country houses were refortified in the 1640s to counter the threat of war and were the scene of numerous military operations during the period as a result of the siege mentality of contemporary society. Examples include Corfe Castle, Dorset, which was besieged twice, the second siege lasting from October 1645 until February 1646, and Lathom House in Lancashire, also twice besieged, on the first occasion from February to May 1644 and on the second from July to December 1645. The building was razed to the ground following the war. In contrast Farnham Castle, Surrey, fell within a few hours on 30th November 1642. The Civil War was the last time that most of these fortifications served a purely military use. The conflict has left its imprint on many structures and the increasing number of excavations carried out on such sites is revealing much new evidence.

Other places which were also fortified and sometimes besieged retain no obvious traces of this period of warfare. Dover Castle, Kent, for example, which has fabric representing almost every period of military history from the Romans to the twentieth century, has no recognisable features relating to the siege of 1648. The reuse of the then relatively recent sixteenth-century coastal fortifications was common during the Civil War. Those at Deal, Walmer and Sandown, all in Kent, were besieged in 1648 while the forts at Pendennis and St Mawes in Cornwall and Calshot in Hampshire were garrisoned and Pendennis was besieged during the war. At none of these does any structural evidence for the reuse during the Civil War exist today.

Earthwork defences

Civil War defence works exist around older castles as a result of the need to improve the original fortifications. As the tall masonry structures of the medieval period offered easy targets for cannon, the garrisons frequently built earthen fortifications to provide some form of additional defence in depth. At Donnington Castle near Newbury in Berkshire the fourteenth-century structure is surrounded by a 'star fort' of four large diamond-shaped earthen bastions connected by several stretches of curtain wall, all built in 1643-4 under the direction of the Royalist officer Colonel John Boys (figures 4 and 5). These works, which were formed by digging deep ditches and throwing the earth inwards, were probably surmounted with wooden palisades originally, although none of the earthworks has been excavated. No fieldwork has been carried out at the site since 1932, when the courtyard of the castle

4. Donnington Castle, Berkshire, and outworks: an aerial view. (Photograph: Cambridge University Collection: copyright reserved.)

5. Donnington Castle, Berkshire; view of the eastern bastion in front of the gatehouse. Note the brickwork repair in the left-hand tower. (Photograph: Peter Harrington.)

was trenched, but the fortifications, the interior of the castle and the surrounding fields would well repay further examination. The remaining gatehouse of the castle displays evidence of the siege of 1645 in the form of a large hole in the staircase tower, probably created by a mortar shell and hastily repaired with brick. The fact that the gatehouse is virtually the only part of the castle still standing attests to the severity of bombardment during the various sieges of the castle during the war.

Similar earthwork defences were built around Raglan Castle in Gwent. Traces of several bastions and ramparts can be seen on the ground but show up more clearly from the air (Kenyon, 1982). As with Donnington, no excavation has been carried out on these defences, which were put to good use during the siege of the castle in 1646. After its capitulation the castle was mutilated and the Great Tower partially demolished. Other evidence of the siege; fragments of cannon shot and part of an iron cannon shot mould, was found when the castle was conserved in the 1940s and 1950s, while the breach in the south-east end of the Office Wing and damage to the Closet Tower were caused by the Parliamentarian guns. The castle motte at Cambridge was refortified and in order to construct a bastioned trace fifteen houses were removed in 1643. Four years later these temporary defences were slighted but the remains of three bastions survive on the east and west sides and particularly on the north, where a fine earthwork stands. External defences also survive at the approaches to King Charles's Castle, Tresco, in the Isles of Scilly, where an irregular bastioned earthwork exists (figure 6).

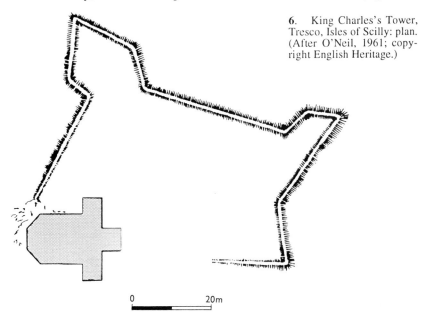

6. King Charles's Tower, Tresco, Isles of Scilly: plan. (After O'Neil, 1961; copyright English Heritage.)

0   20m

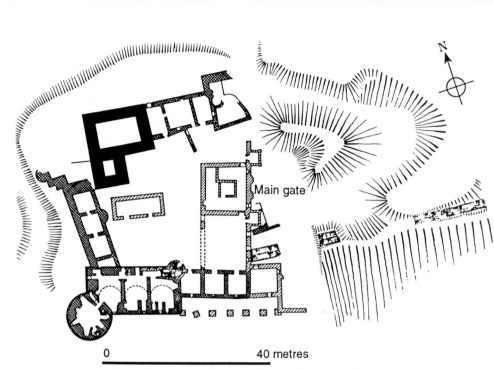

Main gate

0   40 metres

7. (Above) Huntly Castle, Grampian: plan showing the redan in front of the main gate. (Reproduced by courtesy of Historic Scotland.)

There is some evidence for internal rearrangements in castle precincts. At Corfe Castle, Dorset, can be seen the remains of a bastion next to the curtain of the inner ward, built by the garrison to provide an additional platform for artillery. A similar artillery platform was added to the motte at Pontefract, West Yorkshire, and the castle hill at Huntingdon, Cambridgeshire, was also modified. No doubt many castle walls were altered to allow for artillery and close inspection occasionally reveals this. The southern curtains at Chepstow, Gwent, were reinforced and partly rebuilt, with the addition of loopholes for muskets, while the earlier battlements were replaced with stronger parapets to support the use of guns. However, it is not certain whether this was done during the war or following the Restoration.

More interesting alterations to older fortifications survive on the town defences of Berwick-upon-Tweed, Northumberland. Improvements to the massive and lavish Elizabethan defences were apparently continued through the whole of the period of the Civil War and specifically either immediately before an attack on it in 1643 or during its occupation by the Scots until 1645. What survives at Berwick from this period is an earthwork parapet raised on the sentry path along the Elizabethan ramparts and, more impressively, high earthwork gun platforms (technically cavaliers) on the earlier bastions, created in order to improve the field of fire.

Detached outworks

Less extensive detached earthworks exist outside the castle at Huntly, Grampian, in north-east Scotland, where a redan stands to the north-east of the castle gate (figure 7); outside the castle at Sandal, West Yorkshire; in South Wales at the castles of Carew, Manorbier, and Newcastle Emlyn, all in Dyfed, and Caerphilly, Mid Glamorgan; and at Sherborne in Dorset. The gun emplacement at Newcastle Emlyn measures 35 metres by 30 metres and is separated from the outer ward of the castle by a dry moat, which is 7 metres wide and 1 metre deep. Excavation of a ravelin situated in front of the south-west gatehouse of Sherborne Castle proved that it was an artificial platform consisting of 1.83 metres of clay and rock with trenches dug on the north and east sides. The outer defences at Sandal were strengthened by the addition of small bastions, one of which survives in the form of a short bank between two demi-bastions (Mayes and Butler, 1983). At Caerphilly a large redoubt stands near the castle. This high, flat-topped platform, standing over 2 metres above the surrounding ground, measures 45 metres by 36 metres and remains of flat-topped bastions exist on the north and west corners (figure 8). There is evidence for bastions in the other corners. The

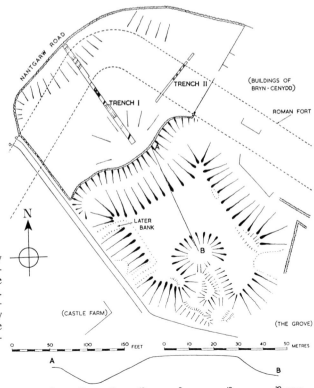

8. (Right) Caerphilly Castle, Mid Glamorgan: plan of the Civil War redoubt. (After Lewis, 1964-6; reproduced by courtesy of the Cambrian Archaeological Society.)

excavator of the site suggested that a large depression measuring 4.2 metres across in the centre of the redoubt may have been for the storage of ammunition, although this feature was not excavated. A ditch surrounds most of the fortification. A further ditch surrounding a mound to the north proved upon excavation to be 6 metres wide and 1.98 metres deep. Seventeenth- and eighteenth-century pottery was found in the ditch. The redoubt, ditches and mound may originally have been an elaborate artillery defence known as a hornwork.

Excavated sites

Civil War levels and features have been located by excavation within the precincts of several castles, most notably at Sandal and Pontefract in West Yorkshire, Corfe in Dorset and Beeston in Cheshire, while similar levels may have been missed during earlier clearance work and limited excavations at many other castles. Additional structures and rearrangements were added to improve defences, as at Wallingford, Oxfordshire, where a stone wall, 1 metre in width and backed by a 2 metre earthen scarp, was added to the medieval defences of the outer ward in 1642. Within the remains of the castle at Bristol there was possible evidence for refortification during the Civil War in the form of

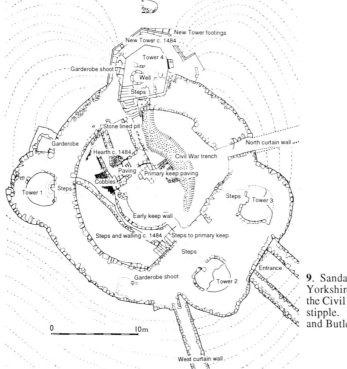

9. Sandal Castle, West Yorkshire: plan. Note the Civil War trench in stipple. (After Mayes and Butler, 1983.)

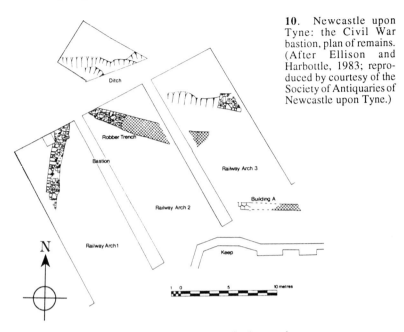

10. Newcastle upon Tyne: the Civil War bastion, plan of remains. (After Ellison and Harbottle, 1983; reproduced by courtesy of the Society of Antiquaries of Newcastle upon Tyne.)

a wall and square tower and the remains of a barrack or armoury.

At Sandal the excavators found that a deep trench had been dug across the top of the twelfth-century motte by the Royalist garrison as a final defensive position during the siege of 1645 (Mayes and Butler, 1983). This enabled the soldiers to communicate between the Well Tower and the Gate Tower in safety (figure 9). By that time the medieval structure had been reduced by bombardment to foundation level. Other masonry structures surmounting the motte had earlier been levelled by the garrison to form gun platforms. Within the fill of the trench large numbers of cannon and musket balls, along with discarded military equipment, were located amongst the collapsed masonry which had fallen into the ditch. The siege lasted almost three months in the summer of 1645 before the Royalist garrison was forced to surrender. Large quantities of military finds, pottery, clay pipes and coins dating from this occupation phase were uncovered. Other evidence for the siege was the pockmarked masonry of the Well Tower, the result of Parliamentarian cannonballs hitting the stonework. Some of these projectiles were found outside this tower. Nine skeletons dating from the Civil War were found at Sandal during the ten years of excavation. Based on the evidence of small pieces of ferrous metal beneath three of the graves, it has been suggested that two of these persons may have been killed by shrapnel from one or more of the mortars which exploded (Manchester, 1979).

Excavations at Newcastle upon Tyne revealed a stone-lined pit beneath the roadway just inside the Black Gate leading into the castle bailey, the probable remains of a new defence system built around the castle in 1642-3 (Ellison *et al*, 1979). This feature, which was approximately 1.3 metres in depth, had been dug into the clay bank of the Norman castle and then lined with stone to form an obstruction squarely across the road. The debris in this pit had started to accumulate during the war and the pottery, consisting mainly of plain-glazed and slip-decorated redwares, tin-glazed wares and bellarmines, along with clay pipes, dates from around 1645 and later. During another excavation in the grounds of the castle the remains of a hastily built 'bastion' were located to the south-west of the Black Gate (Ellison and Harbottle, 1983). These consisted of a stone revetment with a ditch in front of it forming a V-shape (figure 10). The flat-bottomed ditch was revetted with a stone wall 1.2 to 1.4 metres wide, part of which survived to a height of 2 metres. Large quantities of pottery and other artefacts were found but did not contribute to the overall dating of the site although several items — a pottery grenade, a musket rest, musket and pistol balls and three powder holders — suggest that the site was of a military nature (figure 11).

Many spectacular ruins owe their appearance to the deliberate policy of slighting by the Parliamentarians in the years following 1646. In some cases the destruction was extensive, as at Bridgnorth (Shropshire), Caerphilly and Corfe, whereas other structures escaped with only minor damage. The debris from the demolition has preserved the wartime levels at Corfe Castle, where numerous artefacts ranging from spurs and a musket rest to lead shot and cannonballs attest to the siege. Remains of a cavity formed by Parliamentarian sappers in 1646 to demolish the keep can also be seen. Similar evidence of Parliamentarian slighting has been uncovered at Montgomery (Powys) and Beeston castles and important collections of pottery dating from the war have been recovered. At Beeston four sequences of pottery (figure 12) and other artefacts including musket balls were identified in a ditch situated in the inner ward: Civil War occupation layers including those associated with the refurbishing of the defences; Civil War demolition layers; upper Civil War demolition layers; and a post-war level. The excavator suggested that the demolition at Beeston was on a grand scale. At other castles much of the damage was caused by cannon fire or mines during siege operations. The ruined state of the masonry visible on the south-west side of Old Wardour Castle in Wiltshire was caused by mines being detonated during the sieges of the castle, while the tower of

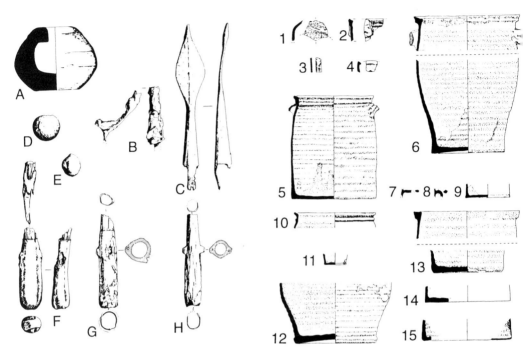

11. (Left) Military finds from Newcastle upon Tyne: A, pottery grenade; B, musket rest; C, iron blade from some form of pole arm; D, musket ball; E, pistol ball; F, G and H, powder holders. (After Ellison and Harbottle, 1983; reproduced by courtesy of the Society of Antiquaries of Newcastle upon Tyne.)

12. (Right) Civil War Pottery from Beeston Castle, Cheshire: 1-9, Civil War occupation; 10-15, Civil War demolition. (After Hough, 1978.)

Ashby de la Zouch Castle, Leicestershire, was split in two. Evidence of damage from bombardment can be seen at many castles such as Skipton in North Yorkshire, Corfe, Donnington and Chepstow, and this is a subject which would repay further examination.

Nottingham Castle was slighted during 1651 after continuous occupation throughout the rebellion. Excavations in Richard's Tower revealed a dense accumulation of rubbish attributed to the Parliamentarian garrison (Drage, 1989). The artefacts recovered were similar to items found elsewhere — a smashed Martincamp flask, large parts of a bellarmine, lead shot, clay-pipe bowls and food debris. Parts of a matchlock were found, along with a wrought iron breech-loading cannon discovered in the well of the tower. Both predated the war and the excavator suggested that such antique weapons may have been used owing to the shortage of arms during the conflict.

Besiegers frequently resorted to mining to destroy walls and gain access to castles. Gunpowder was placed in the tunnels and ignited to bring about the collapse of the masonry. Beleaguered garrisons frequently countermined to combat this threat and archaeological work has turned up evidence of this activity. Excavations within the precincts of Pontefract Castle revealed three countermines. Located at various points just inside the outer walls, they measured about 1.5 metres in diameter and ranged in depth from 3.5 metres to 7 metres. All had penetrated the natural bedrock. They were probably intended as listening galleries to detect the presence of enemy miners. At the base of one shaft was a long pointed iron stake which may have been used for digging through the bedrock, while in the fill of another numerous fragments of wall plaster, some bearing graffiti, drawings and names, were recovered, along with many lead musket balls, clay pipes, pottery and iron fragments from breastplates and helmets.

Fortified houses

Numerous large houses were put into a state of defence during the war and several were subjected to prolonged sieges. At Basing House in Hampshire the remains of at least three earthwork bastions, gun platforms and ditches connected by banks surround the ruins of the sixteenth-century house (figure 13). Located in a strategic position overlooking the main routes to the west, the house was quickly fortified at the outset of the war by the Royalist Marquess of Winchester and was attacked on several occasions, the final siege and assault taking place in the autumn of 1645. A fire destroyed much of the main building following the war and virtually nothing was left standing, hence its appearance today. Later development destroyed further evidence around the site. Excavations commenced as early as the 1870s and have continued intermittently since then. The fact that all occupation ceased after 1645 provides a *terminus post quem* for the artefacts although much of the material dates from the late sixteenth century. Large quantities of pottery and artefacts have been recovered, including parts of matchlock muskets, stirrups and spurs. Excavations in the 1960s revealed a thick ashy layer relating to the war along with hearths and animal bones, some of which were found within a ditch where soldiers may have camped. In the north wing of the 'New House' work revealed a large stable at ground level with living quarters above dating from the war. During excavations of a blocked postern gate in 1991, a skull with a sword slash was found in the central drain of the gate, probably the remains of one of the Royalist defenders (Turton, personal comment). Many of the surviving Tudor outer walls and towers display crude musket loops while in the nearby Grange Barn shot holes can be seen on the north face dating from the Parliamentarian attack of November 1643; the inner face of the same wall bears evidence of the damage resulting from the Royalist counter attack. When the thatch was removed from an adjacent cottage in 1970 numerous musket balls and small round shot were dislodged.

Aerial photography has revealed the remains of two half-moon batteries surrounding Wiverton Hall near Newark and a possible Civil War earthwork might exist at nearby Shelford Manor (RCHM, 1964). Both houses served as Royalist outposts in the area. At Cornbury Park in Oxfordshire the remains of a battery lie close to Cornbury House and it has been suggested that the structure was built early in the war to protect the approaches to the building (O'Neil, 1945).

Other sites, tentatively interpreted as being parts of the defences of country houses during the war, include a possible gun battery at South Kelsey Hall in Lincolnshire, the scene of a minor attack in 1642, and another at Kettlethorpe Hall in the same county, in an area of skirmishing in 1644-5 (RCHME, 1991, 112 and 115).

13. Basing House, Hampshire: aerial view of the house and bastioned defence. (Photograph: Cambridge University Collection: copyright reserved.)

14. The Bulwark, Carmarthen, Dyfed: part of the ditch and rampart. (Photograph: T. A. James, Dyfed Archaeological Trust.)

15. The Queen's Sconce, Newark, Nottinghamshire: aerial view. (Photograph: Cambridge University Collection: copyright reserved.)

4
Town defences

From the largest to the smallest, towns and cities hurriedly constructed obstacles against opponents who might have designs upon them. Many with old walls or earthen banks built additions, created gunports or constructed outworks abutting on to the masonry. Earlier prehistoric and Roman structures were also pressed into service. Inevitably, the standard of construction reflected the differing economic bases of each place.

Few remains of town defences have survived. In the vast majority of cases the fortifications were built of earth, which clearly could not stand the test of time nor survive later urban encroachment. While they were constructed as obstacles to movement, when peace came they still presented a hindrance and were quickly demolished. Many fortifications were removed by order of Parliament to prevent them from being used in any revolt against its rule. At Newark-on-Trent, Nottinghamshire, however, remains of defences, particularly outlying forts, can be seen. At an increasing number of urban sites Civil War fortifications have been located by excavation, although a common phenomenon is the dearth of artefacts as a result of the temporary nature of such defences. Evidence is also being found for the alteration and adaptation of medieval walls during the conflict.

Surface remains

A few vestiges of town defences have survived. For example, on Brandon Hill, Bristol, the remains of a fort can be seen adjoining Cabot Tower and further south is part of an earthen bank 1.2 metres high with two small bastions, one with a half-moon outwork, and a larger bastion known as the Water Fort. These works have survived despite the slighting of the defences in 1647. The fortifications at Bristol were not unlike those constructed around London, Chester, Liverpool and Plymouth, but these have long since gone although excavations have located some of the defences at Plymouth (see below). At London, which had 17 km (11 miles) of fortification, some remains did exist into the nineteenth century, but today only the occasional street name attests to the location of the defences.

At Carmarthen in Dyfed a new enceinte was built outside the perimeter of the medieval wall, and a length of curtain 329 metres long with a ditch, a demi-bastion and the mutilated remains of a bastion survive from them (O'Neil, 1938; figure 14). Discovery of a ditch at the nearby friary may suggest that the Royalists started to build a defensive system at the beginning of the war, but this was superseded by a modern bastioned trace probably built under the guidance of a professional soldier, Colonel Gerard. The finest defences were those around Oxford, which cost over £30,000, but virtually nothing has survived save for small portions to the north-east of the city, which are described in the Royal Commission *Inventory* for the city.

Amongst the best preserved of town defences are those at King's Lynn, Norfolk. There, because the medieval defences were reused and the ditches were then incorporated into the overall drainage system of the low-lying area around, the Civil War defences have survived and can be appreciated. As so often with military works, they were constructed after most of the conflict there was over.

At first, in 1642, the town declared itself for Parliament and the thirteenth-century rampart and ditch on the landward side of the town were merely refurbished. In August 1643 the town reversed its support, appointed a Royalist governor and prepared for a siege. After six weeks of considerable bombardment by Parliamentary forces, the town surrendered. It is a measure of the type of warfare that some sources suggest that, despite the ferocity of the attacks, no one was killed.

Immediately after the siege the Parliamentary forces, apparently using the same military engineer as the Royalists, laid out entirely new defences based on the medieval lines. At least five major bastions were added to the east and complex outworks were constructed to the north and south. The eastern bastions still survive and indicate that, though technically correct in plan, they were very slight in height and could never have consisted of more than a simple bank and ditch.

The finest remains of Civil War fortifications exist at Newark-on-Trent and these have been thoroughly documented (RCHM, 1964). Not only parts of the town defences survive but also siegeworks (see chapter 5). At the outset of the war the medieval walls were in such a bad state of repair that the Royalist garrison built a new defensive perimeter in 1642 and this was added to in subsequent years, so that by 1645, the year of the final siege, the fortifications were described as resembling almost an 'entire sconce'. There was considerable evidence of these in the nineteenth century but later development removed many of the features. Some remains of the town perimeter exist in the grounds of the Friary in the form of an eroded mound, while other embankments survive within the vicinity of Sleaford Road. Beyond the defensive perimeter the garrison constructed several strong forts, one of which survives today (figure 15). Arguably the most impressive Civil War earthwork in Britain, the Queen's Sconce is a star-shaped fort of four bastions covering an area of approximately 1.2 ha and surrounded by a large ditch up to 21 metres wide and from 3.6 metres to 4.6 metres deep.

16. Muskham Bridge, Newark, Nottinghamshire: the Royalist defence work seen from the air. (Photograph: Cambridge University Collection: copyright reserved.)

The whole was probably palisaded and a counterscarp bank on the north-east and south-east may relate to this. Within the ditch the rampart rises to a height of over 7 metres. At the gorges of all four bastions are traces of ramps for hauling up cannon. By the 1950s the site had been damaged but restoration work in 1957 removed trees and bushes and a fence was erected. At Muskham Bridge another Royalist defence work, which was modified later by the attacking Scottish troops, survives (figure 16), while other remains are at Crankley Point. The nearby villages of Balderton, Farndon and Coddington display evidence of embankments built by the Parliamentarians and their Scottish allies.

Excavated sites

Where medieval walls were standing, defenders frequently added artillery emplacements or extended the perimeter with earthen banks. Occasionally masonry walls were constructed, as is shown by the discovery of the Roushill Wall in Shrewsbury, Shropshire (Brown and Watson, 1989). During the war a gap in the old medieval walls of the town was filled by the construction of a wall running approximately 145 metres. However, it is uncertain whether this defence was built by the Royalists before the fall of the town in 1645 or was constructed afterwards by order of Parliament as part of the programme for which £4000 was provided by the government in 1645. It is known that the wall was not completed until 1651. About 13 metres of the wall were examined; the width throughout was 1.65 metres and it survived to at least 1 metre. No datable artefacts were recovered. At Newcastle upon

Tyne the effects of the war on the earlier wall have been identified. Two large stretches of wall at Orchard Street were found to have been rebuilt following the siege of 1644 and the remains of a mine crater at one of the reconstructed breaches were discovered.

At Hull, Humberside, the walls were considered ineffective against artillery, so a second circuit of defences was provided, consisting of an outer moat and rampart adjoining hornworks protecting the main gates. Nothing remains of these although archaeological work at the Mytongate revealed possible traces of the wartime defences outside the gate. The site of the Beverley Gate was discovered in 1986 and, though the masonry structure predated the war, it was the gate where Charles I was forbidden entry by Sir John Hotham in 1642, thus precipitating the conflict.

The city of Worcester had six bastions added to its northern and eastern sides in front of its wall. Parts of the lower courses of the wall along City Walls Road bear traces of sockets which may have held timbers for the Civil War fortifications. To the south of the city, which is overlooked by high ground, the Royalists created a line of embankments and ditches centred upon a new star-shaped earthwork called Fort Royal. Little remains of this site as the bastions have been rounded off to form garden bowers. In 1924 fragments of the ditches which connected it to the city walls were visible. Partial excavations in 1969 failed to locate any features or artefacts. However, evidence of the wartime fortification of the city was identified at the King's School site, where a defensive ditch was sectioned and seventeenth-century pottery retrieved. Another ditch was seen to connect with this feature.

Defensive ditches have been located by excavation at several other towns. At Taunton, Somerset, a large ditch 5 metres wide by 1.5 metres deep was uncovered in 1977 and mid seventeenth-century pottery recovered. It was suggested that this may have been the remains of a defensive line constructed in the vicinity of the former priory by Robert Blake in the spring of 1645. Evidence of a Civil War ditch was uncovered at Devizes, Wiltshire, while at Aylesbury in Buckinghamshire excavations in the grounds of the Prebendal located a defensive ditch which completely disregarded the line of earlier prehistoric and Saxon defences (figure 17). This led the excavator to suggest that it was part of the defences built in 1642 by the Parliamentary garrison.

Similar remains were found at Reading, Berkshire. At the beginning of the war a large continuous enceinte was built connected to a massive fort known as Harrison's Barn. Part of the defences cut through the eastern edge of Reading Abbey and this was found by excavation in 1979 and 1981. The work also uncovered the remains of a massive ditch which may have been an additional part of the defences. In the adjacent Forbury Park a large landscaped mound surmounted by gravel and benches may date from the war although it could equally be an earlier castle motte.

At Abbey Green, Chester, the excavators located a trench running parallel within and about 6 metres from the city wall (Ward, 1987). The 2.5 metre wide trench extended along the whole length of the excavation, a distance of 27 metres, and continued to the west and east of it. The builders of the ditch had cut into medieval, Saxon and Roman levels. Large quantities of seventeenth-century pottery were recovered although there was no material that provided an actual date for the feature, but a date in the 1640s is not inconsistent; clay pipes, four pieces of lead shot, a sandstone projectile and post-medieval glass were recovered from the trench. Early in 1643 directions were given to repair the existing walls and pile up earth against them so as better to absorb the shock from artillery projectiles, and it is probable that this ditch was dug to provide the necessary earth. Parts of the city wall received considerable damage from Parliamentarian guns and several breaches were made, one of which has been identified on a stretch of wall running along the Roman Gardens parallel with Souters Lane. Marks possibly made by enemy cannonballs have been noticed on the Barnaby Tower near the south-east corner of the wall. Close examination revealed twenty circular depressions on the eastern face of the

17. The Prebendal, Aylesbury, Buckinghamshire, excavated in 1985. In the foreground can be seen a section cut across the Civil War defence. The backfilled ditch can be seen running back towards a second cut near the top of the photograph. (Copyright: Buckinghamshire County Museum.)

tower (figure 18). Elsewhere along the wall gunports were created out of medieval embrasures.

The work at Chester has demonstrated the type of evidence left by the war on masonry structures and it serves as an important model for future work in other areas. Elsewhere in the city, at the East Gate, evidence was found for the destruction of buildings during the war and this is a phenomenon that will no doubt be met with elsewhere. For instance, it is known that over 240 houses in the suburbs of Gloucester were destroyed in August 1643 at the commencement of the siege to prevent them from being used by the attacking Royalists, and during excavations on the Bank of England site in Southgate Street the remains of a house which was probably deliberately burnt before the siege were found.

Evidence of circumvallations or trench lines has been found at several places between the centre of Dorchester in Dorset and the outlying fort within the old Roman amphitheatre at Maumbury Rings (see chapter 6). A similar feature was uncovered at Pontefract, West Yorkshire, during excavations on The Booths and Ass Hill. This ditch originally connected the east gate of the castle with All Saints' Church, where the

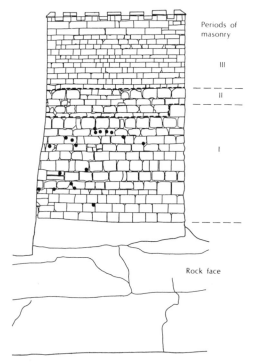

Periods of
masonry

III

II

I

Rock face

18. Barnaby's Tower, Chester, showing the cannonball marks as black dots, all of which are on masonry of the lowest and earliest phase, consisting of large weathered sandstone blocks. The levels of masonry above date from more recent periods. (Reproduced by courtesy of Mr Simon Ward and the Department of Leisure Services, Council of the City of Chester.)

19. Pontefract, West Yorkshire: the siege trench, Tanner's Row, excavated in 1985. Note the wheel ruts. (Photograph: Eric Houlder. Reproduced by courtesy of the West Yorkshire Archaeological Service.)

besieged Royalists had placed a garrison. It took the form of a droveway up to 2 metres in depth. At Ass Hill part of this had been protected with a low stone breastwork. Musket balls were found in the fill and wheel ruts were uncovered along the excavated stretches of the ditch (figure 19). The church fell in June 1645 after two days of heavy bombardment. It was then bombarded by its former defenders and parts of the building are still roofless as a result.

Major excavations on the Civil War defences have been carried out at Gloucester, Exeter and to a lesser extent at Plymouth. Several sites have been excavated at Gloucester (Atkin, 1991). At Southgate Street a ditch dating from 1643 was found and the fill included five hundred clay pipes. The ditch was V-shaped and approximately 5.5 metres wide and 2.3 metres deep (figures 20 and 21). The remains of a bastion in the form of a massive chevron-shaped ditch, 10 metres wide by 4 metres deep, were found in 1983 and 1989 outside the South Gate. At the base of the ditch a wooden structure which may have been part of a cheval-de-frise was recovered. Other possible remains of the wartime defences have been found at St Michael's Square, Wellington Street. Excavation in 1974 on the East Gate revealed evidence for the filling of the gate passage with earth when the ditch was breached during the siege. Lastly the remains of two Royalist sapping mines were found during the work on the Bank of England site in Southgate Street.

Before work commenced at Exeter, Devon, extensive documentary research on the Civil War defences was undertaken (Stoyle, 1988, 1990). Since then, excavations have uncovered remains of the defences in several places. At the ABC cinema site two phases of the defences

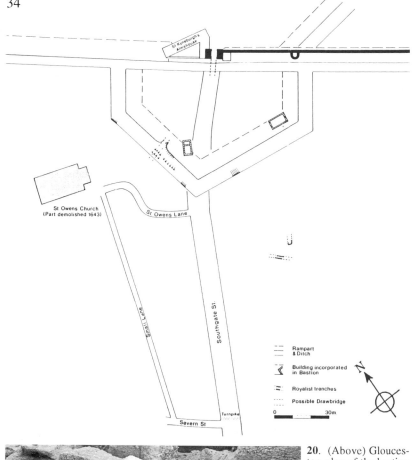

St Kyneburgh's Almshouse

St Owens Church
(Part demolished 1643)

St Owens Lane

Small Lane

Southgate St.

Turnpike

Severn St

Rampart & Ditch

Building incorporated in Bastion

Royalist trenches

Possible Drawbridge

0   30m

N

20. (Above) Gloucester: plan of the bastion constructed around the South Gate in 1642-3, based on the evidence from excavations in 1983-9. (Reproduced by courtesy of Gloucester Excavations Unit.)

21. (Left) Gloucester: a section through the South Gate bastion ditch, excavated in 1983. (Reproduced by courtesy of Gloucester Excavations Unit.)

22. Exeter, Devon: plans of the East Gate defences in 1642-3 and 1644-6, based on evidence from excavations. (Reproduced by courtesy of Exeter Museums Archaeological Field Unit.)

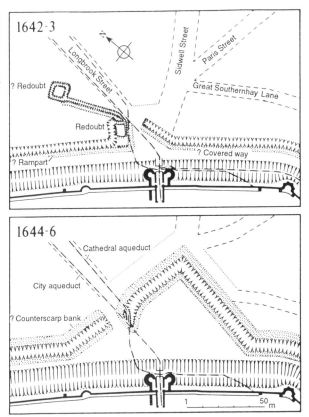

were identified. In the first period a small redoubt was constructed on the edge of a hillside to the west of Longbrook Street. It measured 6 metres by 7.5 metres between the ditches. A hollow way adjacent to this feature was deepened to create a broad ditch about 1.5 metres deep. Civil War ditches have been located at several sites around the city; these include a V-shaped ditch 3 metres wide by 2 metres deep near the South Gate which may have been the remains of a battery. Outside the East Gate a 5 metre wide ditch was located (figure 22). Some of the ditches found at Exeter may have been covered ways. At the Friary Goods Yard site in Plymouth, Devon, two phases of the Civil War defences were found. The first was a turf-revetted bank 7 to 8 metres wide built in the summer of 1643 and the second a stone facing wall and parapet added to the front of the earlier bank shortly thereafter.

York was extensively refortified and was besieged by the Parliamentarians for eleven weeks in 1644. Most traces of the war have been swept away although one site on Baile Hill has produced evidence. The site of a castle motte was modified to accommodate two cannon. Excavations in 1968 and 1969 suggested that the mound had been heightened during the war. A deposit over 1 metre in thickness was found to contain Saxo-Norman pottery, along with ashlar masonry from the city wall, which crosses the mound, and seventeenth-century pottery. One other site is Holgate Hill, which now consists of shapeless fragments in suburban gardens. A plan was made of this site of a Civil War fort in 1904 and it was excavated 32 years later by Corder. A rectangular area approximately 50 metres by 46 metres was surrounded by a slight rampart and ditch and resembled some of the redoubts at Newark built by the Scottish troops. Other forms of evidence exist for the war, such as blocked embrasures creating musket loops, bullet marks south-east of Micklegate Bar, and sagging in the north-east wall of the Barbican, due possibly to Civil War mines. Over the years numerous cannonballs have been found, including one embedded in the wall near Micklegate Bar and two unexploded mortar shells at Walmgate Bar.

At Newark, as with many other towns and cities, the defences and the castle were slighted after the war but this was not completed because of an outbreak of plague. Besides the visible earthworks referred to before, evidence of the defences has been revealed by excavation at several sites in the town. At Millgate a series of beam slots was found averaging 0.65 metre in width, 0.10 metre in depth and almost 0.20 metre apart. These may have been the remains of timbers revetting a gravel rampart forming a hornwork, serving also to support the rampart under the weight of cannon (Dean, 1968). Small amounts of seventeenth-century and earlier pottery were also recovered. At nearby Victoria Street excavations in 1986 uncovered a large ditch, which was examined in three places. It measured 3.4 metres wide and over 1.8 metres deep and was dug into the natural gravel. In the secondary filling a small number of seventeenth-century pottery sherds were recovered, as were a few metal items including a bronze stirrup. From the limited evidence the excavator concluded that the ditch represented part of the south-west circuit of the Royalist defences constructed in 1643-4, and that it was probably deliberately filled during the slighting operations following the war (Drage, 1987). In the following year a large ditch measuring 1.5 metres deep and 2 metres wide was exposed during building operations close to Victoria Street. A site of a possible redoubt was excavated in 1988 close to the village of Winthorpe near Newark but no conclusive evidence was forthcoming.

5
Siegeworks and forts

As with town defences, most of the fortifications thrown up by besieging armies during the English Civil War have been destroyed. For instance, near Donnington Castle, Berkshire, traces of a Parliamentarian battery were visible in the nineteenth century on nearby Snelsmore Heath. At Basing House, Hampshire, the ploughed-out remains of a bank and ditch, possibly representing the Parliamentarian circumvallation constructed around the house, were noted in April 1953 stretching in a direct line for nearly 1 km. They were less than 30 metres from the salient angle of the southern bastion (O'Neil, 1960). The sites which have survived consist in the main of batteries hastily built to accommodate various artillery pieces. While some reflect contemporary principles of siege warfare, others are crude enclosures or barricades, and today it is often difficult to determine whether they are from the war. Infrequency of occupation has left little in the way of datable artefacts. Other means of dating such as documentary evidence or place-name survivals may be used, although the latter should be treated with caution.

Siegework remains

The 1646 siege of Raglan Castle in Gwent is represented by a small pentagonal earthwork with a salient pointing towards the castle on a slight rise about 216 metres east-northeast of the castle (Kenyon, 1982). On the ground a shallow ditch can be made out in front of a concrete reservoir but from the air the siegework can be clearly seen (figure 23). This may have been the site of Morgan's Battery, which was constructed to fire at the towers of the castle. At Park Hill, Skipton, in North Yorkshire, a small rectangular earthwork, measuring approximately 21 square metres and surrounded by a ditch, lies some 360 metres north-west of the castle. Inside the ditch on the south is a slight rampart. A small excavation of the site in 1937 revealed little other than two fragments of mid seventeenth-century glass from the rampart. This battery was one of several built by the Parliamentarians during the siege of the castle which lasted from 1642 to 1645. Remains of one artillery platform near the Gargrave Road were visible in the late nineteenth century while the location of a third site has been recorded at Cock Hill, where a stirrup was found in 1877. Cannonballs, presumably fired from the castle, occasionally turn up in the Eller Beck stream below this site. A Parliamentary battery at Galch Hill near Bryn Park, Denbigh, Clwyd, was constructed to attack the castle, while below the Goblin Tower of the town wall a siegebank or mount exists. A small

earthwork known as Prince Rupert's Mount lies on the edge of a modern housing estate overlooking Lichfield Cathedral close in Staffordshire (figure 24). This is the site of a battery built during the attack on
the city in 1643.

Siegeworks thrown up around towns have mostly been destroyed by
slighting or urban growth but a few survive. In the meadows beside the
river Dee at Chester, in an area known as Earl's Eye, there are traces of
a rectangular enclosure which may be the remains of the Lower Mount
built by the Parliamentarian troops when besieging the city in 1645
(Ward, 1987). Excavations near the South Gate, Gloucester, have revealed traces of Royalist siege trenches (figure 25). Several earthworks

23. Raglan Castle, Gwent: aerial view showing the Parliamentary siegework in the centre
of the photograph. (Photograph: Cambridge University Collection: copyright reserved.)

24. Prince Rupert's Mount, Lichfield, Staffordshire: the site of a battery built in 1643. (Photograph: Peter Harrington.)

25. Gloucester: view of the base of a Royalist sap lying outside the South Gate; excavated in 1988. (Reproduced by courtesy of Gloucester Excavations Unit.)

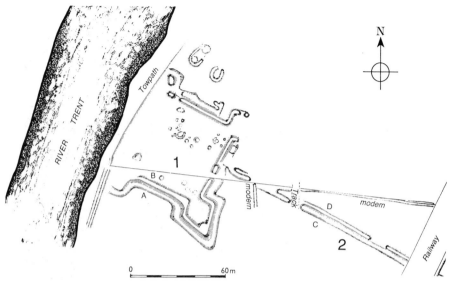

26. Crankley Point, Newark, Nottinghamshire: plan of the earthworks, including Colonel Gray's Sconce. (After RCHM, *Newark*, 1964; reproduced by courtesy of the Royal Commission on the Historic Monuments of England.)

have been identified as Parliamentarian siegeworks around Newark. Colonel Gray's Sconce, for example, was built beside the river Trent to protect a bridge of boats across the river connecting the Parliamentarians with their Scottish allies (figure 26). While most of the site was destroyed in 1960, excavations two years earlier did recover some information about the internal layout. The site had been a square fort covering an area of almost 0.40 ha, with bastions at two corners and demi-bastions at the others. The sides of the earthwork between the bastions measured 46 metres (figure 27). Excavations were made in two places, on the gun platform of the south-east bastion and in the centre of the southern side; these showed that the ditch had been originally over 1.5 metres deep, while five postholes set at 0.60 metre intervals were located along the scarp but not on the bastion (Manning, 1958; figure 28). A rough firestep was noticed along the side of the fort and within the work were shallow pits which may have been the sites of bivouacs. Running into the earthwork on the south-east side was a ditch measuring over 150 metres. This represented part of the circumvallation built by the besiegers around Newark and consisted of a bank and ditch with an overall width of 7.6 metres. It too was examined in 1958 and was found to be just over 1 metre in depth,

27. (Right) Colonel Gray's Sconce, Newark, Nottinghamshire: aerial view. (Photograph: Cambridge University Collection: copyright reserved.)

28. (Below) Sections through the earthworks of Colonel Gray's Sconce, Newark (1), and the line of circumvallation (2). See figure 26 for the locations of 1 and 2. (After RCHM, *Newark*, 1964; reproduced by courtesy of the Royal Commission on the Historic Monuments of England.)

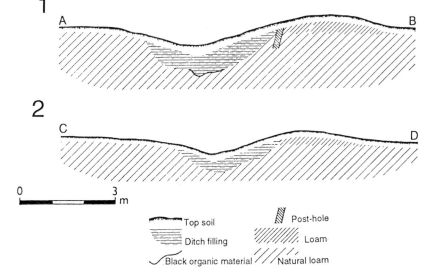

1

A   B

2

C   D

0   3   m

Top soil   Post-hole

Ditch filling   Loam

Black organic material   Natural loam

29. Hawton, near Newark, Nottinghamshire: aerial view of the Civil War redoubt inside an earlier moated site. (Photograph: Cambridge University Collection: copyright reserved.)

30. Earith Bulwark, Cambridgeshire: aerial view. (Crown Copyright 1991/MOD; reproduced with the permission of the Controller of HMSO.)

although it probably had been intended to be deeper. There was no evidence of palisading. The circumvallation has shown up elsewhere around the town (RCHM, 1964).

Other siegeworks at Newark consist of a redoubt built within the earthworks of a medieval moat at Hawton (figure 29) and several works constructed by the Scottish troops, including a bastion of a large fort called Edinburgh at Kelham, the Sandhills Sconce, a fort at Stoke Lodge and several smaller earthworks. However, of all the sites around Newark only Colonel Gray's Sconce has been excavated.

One remarkable survival of a siegework is at Colchester, Essex. The complex and elaborate siegeworks laid out in 1648 during the siege by Parliamentary forces have mostly been destroyed by later housing development and agricultural changes. An exception, however, is one small fort on the east side of the town. On an air photograph taken by Professor J. K. St Joseph in 1949 the cropmarks of a star-shaped fort are visible, together with the line of a ditch which may be the associated covered way.

Another single remnant of what were presumably complex siegeworks is at King's Lynn, Norfolk. There, in the marshes to the north-east of the town, the modern pattern of drainage ditches at one point describes the shape of a perfect bastion. They thus mark one side of a small fort, presumably dating from the 1643 siege.

Most of the Parliamentarian siegeworks at York have long gone although the site of one battery exists at Lamel Hill south-east of the Walmgate Bar. Today the hill is flat-topped, measures 31 metres in diameter and is surmounted by a summerhouse. Excavations in 1849 revealed that the upper 3 to 4 metres of the mound contained human bones from an early Christian cemetery, but also post-medieval coins and a seventeenth-century storage jar. Other than this, there was little evidence for its use during the war.

Independent forts and batteries

Many of the better preserved sites of the war are found in rural areas, having been built to guard strategic roads or river crossings. Two of the finest sites are in Cambridgeshire, at Earith and Horsey Hill. The fort at Earith was constructed by the Parliamentarians to guard the river crossing over the Ouse and the Old Bedford River (figure 30). It has been suggested that the fort was designed by Captain John Hopes and Richard Clamp. Covering nearly 2 ha, it consists of a square earthwork with angular bastions at each corner, the whole surrounded by a ditch. A rampart runs around the top of the work. On the western side are two parallel ditches which run over 80 metres away from the fort and may have served as an outwork (figure 31). Small-scale excavations in 1908

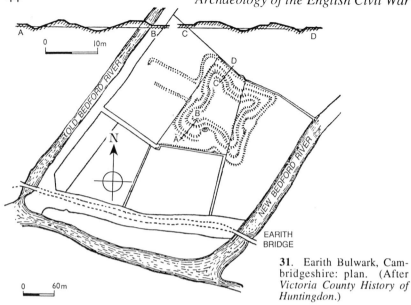

31. Earith Bulwark, Cam-
bridgeshire: plan. (After
*Victoria County History of
Huntingdon.*)

revealed very little about the origins of the site (Keynes and White,
1908). A trench was cut through the western face of the north-west
bastion and the rampart was found to measure over 9 metres in thickness and 2.4 metres above the old ground surface. A further trench was
dug from the rampart to the bottom of the ditch and a final excavation
was made in the centre of the fort with little result, leading the excavators to conclude that occupation of the site had been short.

Further north, on the road from Peterborough to Whittlesey, the fort
at Horsey Hill commands the crossing of the river Nene (figure 32). It
covers about the same area as the Earith Bulwark but is pentagonal
rather than square, with bastions at each corner. A continuous rampart
extends over 4 metres above the bottom of the surrounding ditch and
the only break in the bank is in the centre of the southern curtain where
the entrance was located. No excavation has been carried out on the
site, which also contains farm buildings within its perimeter.

Two batteries, both at locations where troops were assembled, are at
Newport Pagnell, Buckinghamshire, and Leverington, Cambridgeshire.
At Newport Pagnell a raised diamond-shaped mound in the churchyard
is probably a battery designed to cover the crossing of the river Ouse,
while a round mound with ramped access at Leverington seems to be
covering an area otherwise protected by the broad curve of the old river
Nene.

Another isolated battery, usually described as a sconce, survives in the centre of a modern housing estate on the outskirts of Huntingdon, Cambridgeshire. It is now very slight and somewhat battered but it is protected as a scheduled ancient monument. Its original function seems to have been to protect the eastern approaches to the town by road and perhaps also by river.

Seemingly isolated are two forts on the Isle of Man. In the centre of the island lies a restored square bastioned defence work known as Fort Loyal, probably built by the Royalist Earl of Derby in 1648-9. To the south lies a less impressive earthwork at Bishopscourt, with a ditch measuring 6.3 metres wide and 1.2 metres deep and bastions at the north-west and north-east corners (Curphey, 1974). A horseshoe-shaped earthwork halfway along the south-west side may be the remains of a hornwork guarding the entrance. It was built as a defence around the Bishop's House, which had been retained by the Earl of Derby after 1643.

Three other sites worthy of mention are the battery overlooking the Great North Road at Sawtry, Cambridgeshire (figure 33), the 'fort' at March in the same county, and the redoubt on top of Burnswark, Dumfries and Galloway. On Tout Hill, Sawtry, lies an embanked platform within a larger embanked and ditched enclosure. The site was initially

32. Horsey Hill, Cambridgeshire: aerial view of the fort. (Photograph: Cambridge University Collection: copyright reserved.)

thought to have been of Roman origin but a small excavation in three places suggested a date later than the thirteenth century and when the site was surveyed it was found to resemble a gun platform of the seventeenth century. An ambiguous site at March consists of a rectangular enclosure surrounded by a ditch and standing only 1 metre above the surrounding land. Bastions exist on the south-east and the north-east corners but a rampart is absent. As the site was clearly unfinished and built in a location with no apparent military importance, it has been suggested that it was built by amateur soldiers as a training exercise. The redoubt on Burnswark was partially excavated during work on the hillfort and Roman site (Jobey, 1973). The structure measured almost 40 metres across and resembles two demi-bastions back to back surrounded by a ditch. Two entrances were examined, as well as a large part of the interior. As with similar sites, contemporary artefacts were scarce, the only related items being part of a clay-pipe stem, some runnels of lead which may have been for the manufacture of musket shot, and one gunflint. The earthwork compares with the sites of Pellew's Redoubt, Toll's Island, in the Scillies, and Baile Hill, York.

Documentary evidence, coupled with an understanding of seventeenth-century communications in terms of roads and river crossings and the strategic thinking of the armies, will no doubt lead to the identification of additional sites in the future.

33. Sawtry, Cambridgeshire: aerial view of the battery overlooking the Great North Road. (Photograph: Cambridge University Collection: copyright reserved.)

6
Other sites and evidence

Island and coastal fortifications

Civil War sites have been found on coastal and island sites, particularly in south-west England and the Isle of Man. The Royalist cause received much of its material and financial support from the continent and this lifeline had to be protected from the Parliament-controlled navy. Much of this clandestine activity required safe havens for loading and unloading cargoes. As the war progressed, much of the navy changed sides and was reorganised by the Royalists to attack Parliamentarian ships, and island refuges were ideal places from which to mount raids against enemy shipping. Three islands or island groups in particular have produced considerable evidence of defensive measures taken during the war: Lundy, strategically situated off the north coast of Devon and in the approaches to the Bristol Channel; the Isle of Man, located midway between Britain and Ireland; and the various islands which make up the Scillies off the Cornish coast.

These sites present problems for the archaeologist, not the least being identification, since few conform to any standard principle of fortification but rather they resemble hastily built platforms. Similarly, breastworks take the form of crude barricades, frequently taking advantage of natural features and local building materials. Whether these sites were occupied for any length of time is open to conjecture but, as many are found on cliff tops where soils are thin, few deposits are likely to have survived.

On Lundy three batteries probably dating from the war have been identified at Brazen Ward, North End and Marisco Castle. Other battery sites exist but some may date from the previous century. It is known that the Royalist commander, Thomas Bushell, had fortifications built around the island before the place was finally forced to surrender in February 1647. The feature at Brazen Ward consists of a line of drystone walling built of large granite boulders but resembling no particular form, the outline of a small breastwork and the foundations of a small dwelling. It was enough, however, to accommodate a cannon to guard the approach to a landing place. The situation on Lundy is paralleled on the Isle of Man, where the Earl of Derby built several coastal emplacements around the north of the island near Ramsey. Some of these continued in use following the war and the remains of several have been identified (Curphey, 1967).

By far the largest group of sites dating from the war survives on the Isles of Scilly. Many breastworks, batteries and platforms built by the

Royalists dot the islands of St Mary's, Tresco, Bryher, Samson, St Agnes and Gugh. These crude defences represent local adaptations at a time of emergency. Today many are threatened by beach erosion and several surveys have been made to determine their form before they are destroyed. One site on Tresco, known as Oliver's Battery, has been consolidated to prevent further erosion (Ratcliffe and Sharp, 1990). The site consists of an earth and stone bank incorporating natural rocks and measuring 9 to 13 metres wide by 0.4 to 1.3 metres high internally and 2.9 to 4.5 metres high externally. Along the west and south sides is a ditch. A break in the bank on the south-east corner may represent an embrasure for a gun (figure 34).

Coastal fortifications survive along the coastline of south-west England, particularly around the important Dart and Fal rivers. Some of the defences built around Pendennis Castle at Falmouth, Cornwall, survive (Johnson, personal comment) and at the nearby Helford river a small bastioned fort on Dennis Head is in a good state of preservation. Besides the two sixteenth-century castles at the mouth of the river Dart in Devon, two earthwork forts were built by the Royalists in 1645; the one on the western bank, known as Gallant's Bower, can still be seen.

Reused sites

As many early sites, and prehistoric structures particularly, were built in commanding positions, it is no surprise to find that some were adapted and reused for service in the Civil War. Allcroft mentions that several prehistoric camps in southern England were occupied during the war, and at Castle Hill, East Retford, Nottinghamshire, the bank of a prehistoric earthwork was heightened and the ditch re-dug by the Parliamentarians to create a fortification to observe movements along the Great North Road and around Newark (Gaunt, 1987). Archaeological and documentary evidence suggests that the two prehistoric sites of Castilly and Castle Dore in Cornwall were used during the 1640s. Wheel ruts possibly made by heavy guns were found during excavations at Castilly henge and the excavator suggested that the southern end of the site had been modified. The iron age hillfort of Castle Dore was occupied in 1644 and, while a few relics were found during excavations in 1950, there was no evidence for modifications to the site during the Civil War.

At several places earlier structures were used to mount cannon during siege operations. At Laugharne Castle in Dyfed the besiegers placed a battery on a prehistoric or Romano-British enclosure situated on a cliff-edge to attack the eastern side of the inner ward in 1644. A second example is at Corfe Castle, Dorset, where the Parliamentarian troops adapted the remains of a ring and bailey castle known as The Rings or Cromwell's Battery, situated 300 metres south-west of the castle. This

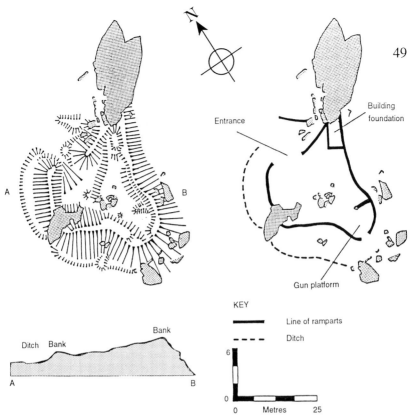

34. Oliver's Battery, Tresco, Isles of Scilly: plans. (After Ratcliffe and Sharp, 1990; reproduced by courtesy of the Cornwall Archaeological Unit.)

site had probably been built as a siegework against the castle in 1139 so it was natural for the seventeenth-century soldiers to adapt it for their use. A rampart walk inside the bank could represent this reuse. There is evidence for modifications made during the war to the Norman mottes at Ailey Hill near Ripon, North Yorkshire, Baile Hill, York, and Hunting-don Castle, Cambridgeshire (figure 35). At Cambridge the eleventh-century motte overlooking the town was adapted to become one of the bastions of the fort there. The rearward ramp leading to the summit of the motte is presumably a Civil War access for cannon.

By far the strongest evidence for reuse of an earlier site comes from Maumbury Rings in Dorchester, Dorset, where the surviving earth-works and the archaeological evidence both point to Civil War occupa-tion (Bradley, 1975). A neolithic henge which was later built over by the Romans to create a small amphitheatre, this site was modified by the Parliamentarians with the addition of ramps and an artillery plat-form to command the Weymouth road. Work began in July 1642 and the modifications included an internal platform and terrace, presumably

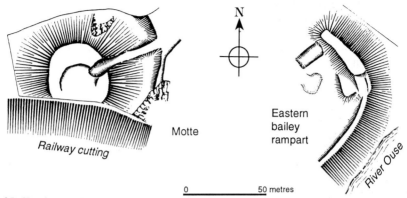

35. Huntingdon Castle, Cambridgeshire: plan of the Civil War modifications to the castle motte. (After Taylor, 1974.)

to facilitate hauling cannon up on to the work, and a gun platform at the south-west. Excavations between 1908 and 1913 produced over 160 lead pistol bullets from the east bank while seventeenth-century pottery came from the area of the gun platform (figure 36). Excavation of the area immediately outside the entrance revealed a narrow-bottomed ditch between 1.8 and 2.4 metres wide and from 0.76 to 1.2 metres deep at three points along the edge of the outer bank. The soil from this ditch had been thrown up on to the main Roman bank. This may have been the remains of a communication trench around the entire structure and it appears to have connected to a V-shaped ditch forming an additional defence, 2.9 metres wide by 1.8 metres deep. Immediately to the east of this second feature were found the remains of yet another trench, leading in the direction of the south gate of the town. This same trench was located at other sites further north (Bradley, 1975).

Battlefields

Over the years numerous items have been found at several battlefields while illegal use of metal detectors has no doubt accounted for many artefacts. A number of relics from the battlefield of Edgehill in Warwickshire have been recorded, including numerous musket balls weighing on average just over 28 grams. Some showed signs of the bullet mould in the form of a line around the circumference. Larger bullets and cannonballs have also been found. One weighed approximately 4.5 kg and may have been fired by a Royalist demi-cannon. Most of the musket balls and cannonballs did not fall into standard calibres and probably represent improvisation by both armies. Other artefacts include iron nails, a horseshoe, a rim tyre of a heavy vehicle, a spear or pike head and some swords (Young, 1967).

Few battlefields have been subjected to modern survey methods, the one exception being Marston Moor in North Yorkshire, although Naseby in Northamptonshire has been fieldwalked. Between 1973 and 1979 a research project was conducted at Marston Moor by Dr Peter Newman and Mr V. R. Cammidge to determine the course of the action from the location of relics and their relative densities (Newman, 1980). This involved extensive fieldwalking and mapping in conjunction with documentary evidence and has resulted in the discovery of several thousand individual bullets. For instance, during the levelling of a field bank in the 1960s, hundreds of musket balls were found, representing the intense fire from the Royalists against the advancing enemy. This work has allowed the researchers to reconstruct points of intense fire. Likewise, the numerous horseshoes found in specific areas may show patterns of cavalry movement. Other artefacts have included musket fittings, sword fragments, lead tokens and a few coins. Some of the

36. Maumbury Rings, Dorchester, Dorset: plan showing Civil War features. (After Bradley, 1975; reproduced by courtesy of the Society of Antiquaries.)

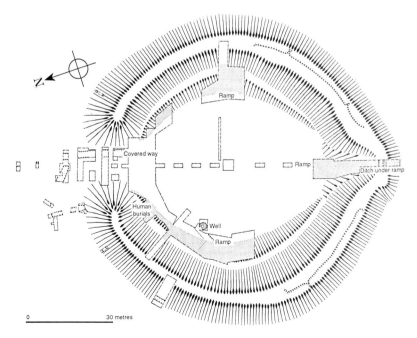

bullets were flattened or hammered, presumably to create some lethal effect, while other bullets had human teeth marks in them which might point to 'biting the bullet' by wounded men undergoing surgery, or to having been held in the mouth by musketeers before being loaded. Other balls had been fused together, suggesting that two or more bullets had been rammed into the musket barrel. The work at Marston Moor demonstrates the importance of battlefield archaeology and the kinds of evidence available and can be used as a model for surveys of other battlefields.

Burials

The only large cemetery dating from the Civil War has been found at Abingdon in Oxfordshire although a small cemetery has been excavated in Edinburgh Castle. Almost 250 burials were examined at Abingdon out of a total of possibly five hundred. All were spaced in regular rows and contained skeletons of both sexes. The fact that the burials were orientated north-south suggests that the cemetery ceased to be used after 1663 when the Anglican burial rite became law. One skeleton from a mass grave containing nine male bodies had a musket ball between its ribs, while coins of the period were found in other graves. At Edinburgh sixteen graves of young males, some of whom exhibited evidence of traumatic injuries which had healed, were found. The cemetery may date from the period of the Cromwellian garrison of the castle around 1650. During excavations within the Elizabethan chapel at Pontefract Castle six Civil War graves were found. With the help of documentary evidence, the archaeologists surmised that following the capture of nearby All Saints' Church by the enemy the Royalist garrison was forced to bury its dead within the confines of the castle. In the area of the Castle Green at Nottingham the remains of a young adult between 25 and 30 years of age were uncovered. While he may have been a Civil War fatality, there was no sign of violence to the bones. Nine skeletons dating from the war were found during the excavations at Sandal Castle, West Yorkshire. A burial from Beeston Castle, Cheshire, apparently had a bullet hole in the head (Kenyon, personal comment). Military burials of the period do show up in parish registers.

Burials have occasionally been found on battlefields. During drainage operations in 1858 and 1859 at Marston Moor certain mounds were explored and at a depth of about 1.2 metres hundreds of skeletons were reportedly found. At Naseby in Northamptonshire a site reported to be a communal grave from the 1645 battle was dug into in the nineteenth century and many skeletons were found. At Worcester two shallow depressions which may have marked burial pits from the 1651 battle were visible in the 1900s on Powick Ham.

Coin hoards

It is generally agreed that warfare and conditions of conflict lead to increased numbers of coin hoards, as people fleeing from danger strive to conceal their valuables until they can be retrieved. While some hoards contain coinage from earlier periods, they usually reflect the currency of the time when they were hidden. The Civil War is no exception and over 115 hoards dating from the period 1639-49 have been found (Besly, 1990). One example comes from Weston-sub-Edge in Gloucestershire, where a hoard was discovered in 1981 during building work at the village hall (Mayhew and Viner, 1987). A lead pipe sealed at both ends contained 307 silver and two gold coins stacked together with a scrap of paper bearing possibly the sum total of the contents. The majority of the coins had been struck in London, where the Tower mint was controlled by Parliament, but there were some interesting finds including two Scottish coins and several examples from the Royalist mint at New Inn Hall Street, Oxford, bearing the inscription 'May God rise up and his enemies be scattered'. Research on the coins suggested a likely date of the summer of 1643 for the hoard.

Because certain towns minted their own siege money during the latter part of the war the coinage of the period is particularly interesting. This currency was issued to beleaguered garrisons to maintain their pay and upkeep. At Pontefract the Royalist garrison during the third siege of 1648 was issued with small lozenges cut from silver plate, to the values of one shilling and two shillings. Some of these have been recorded from excavations within the castle precincts. The siege money from Newark-on-Trent was also lozenge-shaped and dated from 1645. It too was struck from silver plate although this was not municipal plate but probably rolled-out sheets. Scarborough, Carlisle and Colchester also minted siege currency (Besly, 1990).

Ireland

Although Ireland is strictly beyond the scope of this book, it is worth noting that because of the frequent military campaigns between 1602 and 1691 there are more seventeenth-century fortifications there than in the rest of the British Isles. The Confederate Wars of 1642-7 and Cromwell's campaign in Ireland (1649), which was an extension of the English Civil War, produced numerous fortifications and the succeeding period of Cromwellian occupation in the 1650s added to this number. Town defences were built, castles refortified and forts constructed at strategic places. Details of seventeenth-century fortifications in Ireland and information about surviving remains have been listed by Kerrigan (1980), but very few have been excavated.

7
Glossary

Bastion: a strong point along the line of or at the corners of a defensive work, arrow-shaped in plan and designed to provide flanking cover along the adjacent defences or curtain.

Cheval-de-frise: wooden obstacle consisting of squared beams connected to stakes and designed to slow down or halt advancing troops.

Circumvallation: a line of siegeworks which faces open country.

Covered way: communication route, either a walkway or ditch, protected by a rampart.

Curtain: run of wall or rampart between towers and/or bastions.

Demi-bastion: half a bastion (*qv*): that is, half an arrow shape in plan with only one forward face and one flank.

Enceinte: main line of bastions and curtain, particularly of a fortified town, as distinct from outworks.

Flank: length of defence facing towards adjacent defences, from which to provide covering fire. The straight outer sides of a bastion are joined to the adjacent defence line by a flank.

Fort: detached stronghold with provision for flank defence.

Hornwork: defensive work projecting from the main defences and consisting of a short length of curtain set between two demi-bastions. The latter were usually linked back to the main defences by straight sides.

Ravelin: an outwork, V-shaped in plan, always set in front of, and usually below, the main defence curtain.

Redan: a detached outwork, V-shaped in plan with an open rearward side.

Redoubt: a detached outwork, usually rectangular in plan and enclosed on all sides. It usually forms part of a larger system of defence.

Sconce: a detached defensive work or fort with corner bastions.

Slighting: intentional demolition of buildings or defences.

Trace: the plan of a defence work.

8
Sites to visit

The following is a selection of sites to visit with identification of site, national grid reference and published reference. Additional sites are listed in Harrington (1987) and Gaunt (1987). The sites are given in alphabetical order.

The following abbreviations are used in relation to publications:

AA	*Archaeologia Aeliana*
Arch	*Archaeologia*
Arch Camb	*Archaeologia Cambrensis*
Arch J	*Archaeological Journal*
CA	*Carmarthenshire Antiquary*
Oxon	*Oxoniensia*
PCAS	*Proceedings of the Cambridgeshire Antiquarian Society*
PDNHAS	*Proceedings of the Dorset Natural History and Archaeological Society*
PHFCAS	*Proceedings of the Hampshire Field Club and Archaeological Society*
PMA	*Post-Medieval Archaeology*
RCHM	Royal Commission on Historical Monuments
TDGNHAS	*Transactions of the Dumfries and Galloway Natural History and Antiquarian Society*
TS	*Thoroton Society Transactions*
YAJ	*Yorkshire Archaeological Journal*
YAYAS	*Yorkshire Architectural and York Archaeological Society*

ENGLAND

Avon

Bristol, Brandon Hill and Queen's Parade, earthwork enceinte; ST 579728; O'Neil (1960), 89-90.

Over, The Vineyard, bastioned fort; SO 814198; O'Neil (1960), 97; Atkin (1991), 35.

Berkshire

Donnington Castle, Newbury, earthwork defences; SU 461694; O'Neil (1960), 96-7.

Cambridgeshire

Cambridge Castle, earthwork bastions; TL 446593; RCHM, *Cambridge II*, 309.

Earith Bulwark, fort; TL 393750; RCHM, *Hunts*, 310-11.
Horsey Hill, fort; TL 224960; O'Neil (1960); RCHM, *Hunts*, 248.
March, sconce; TL 420957; Brown and Taylor, *PCAS*, 70 (1980), 113-15.

Cornwall and Isles of Scilly
Tresco, King Charles's Castle, earthwork defences; SW 883162; O'Neil (1961), 32; Miles and Saunders, *PMA*, 4 (1970), 1-30.

Devon
Dartmouth, Gallant's Bower fort; SX 884504; O'Neil *Arch*, 85 (1936), 129.

Dorset
Dorchester, Maumbury Rings, gun platform and ramps; SY 691899; Bradley, *Arch*, 105 (1975), 1-97.
Sherborne Old Castle, redan; ST 647167; O'Neil (1960), 107.

Hampshire
Basing House, earthwork defences, musket loops; SU 663527; O'Neil (1960), 94.

North Yorkshire
Skipton, Park Hill, battery; SD 989524; O'Neil (1960), 107.
York, Baile Hill, modified motte; SE 603513; Addyman, *Arch J*, 134 (1977), 115-56.

Nottinghamshire
Newark-on-Trent, Crankley Lane, raised battery; SK 789559; RCHM, *Newark*, 34.
Newark-on-Trent, Muskham Bridge, sconce; SK 786563; RCHM, *Newark*, 34.
Newark-on-Trent, Queen's Sconce, fort; SK 791531; RCHM, *Newark*, 31.

Oxfordshire
Cornbury Park, battery; SP 357184; O'Neil, *Oxon*, X (1945), 73-8.

ISLE OF MAN

Bishopscourt, fort; SC 328924, Curphey, *PMA*, 8 (1974), 104-7.
Fort Loyal, Ballachurry, fort; SC 406970; Gaunt (1987), 91-3.

SCOTLAND

Dumfries and Galloway
Burnswark Hill, redoubt; NY 185786; Jobey, *TDGNHAS*, L (1973), 72-81.

Grampian
Huntly Castle, ravelin; NJ 532408; O'Neil (1960), 103.

WALES

Clwyd
Denbigh, Goblin Tower, siegebank; SJ 052658; Gaunt (1987), 176.

Dyfed
Carew Castle, redan; SN 047038; Gerard, *Fortress*, 6 (1990), 49-50.
Carmarthen, earthwork enceinte; SN 412200; O'Neil, *Arch Camb*, 93 (1938), 126-30.
Manorbier Castle, redan; SN 064978; King, *Arch Camb*, 119 (1970), 83-118.
Newcastle Emlyn Castle, redan; Parry, *CA*, 22 (1987), 14.

Gwent
Raglan Castle, earthwork defences and siegework; SO 418084; Kenyon, *Arch Camb*, 132 (1982), 139-42; Kenyon (1988).

Mid Glamorgan
Caerphilly Castle, redoubt; ST 155873; Lewis, *Arch Camb*, 115 (1964-6), 67-87.

9
Excavated sites

The abbreviations used for publications are explained at the beginning of chapter 8.

ENGLAND

Avon
Bristol Castle; *PMA*, 4 (1970), 174.

Berkshire
Reading Abbey; Vince, Fasham and Hawkes, *Berkshire Archaeological Journal*, 71 (1981-2), 37-9.

Buckinghamshire
Aylesbury, Prebendal grounds; Farley, *Current Archaeology*, 101 (1986), 189.

Cambridgeshire
Earith Bulwark; Keynes and White, *PCAS*, 50 (1908), 257-61.
Sawtry; Tebbutt and Rudd, *PCAS*, 59 (1966), 138-9.

Cheshire
Beeston Castle; Hough, *Journal of the Chester Archaeological Society*, 61 (1978), 1-23.
Chester, Abbey Green; Ward (1987).

Cornwall
Castilly; Thomas, *Cornish Archaeology*, 3 (1964), 3-14.

Devon
Exeter, ABC cinema site; *PMA*, 23 (1989), 29-32.
Exeter, Trinity Lane; *PMA*, 24 (1990), 161-3.
Plymouth, Friary Goods Yard; *PMA*, 24 (1990), 163-4.

Dorset
Corfe Castle; Thackray and Papworth, *PDNHAS*, 108 (1986) to 113 (1991).
Dorchester, Eldridge Pope's Brewery; *PDNHAS*, 73 (1951), 101.
Dorchester, Maumbury Rings; Bradley, *Arch*, 105 (1975), 1-97.
Sherborne Castle; *PDNHAS*, 63 (1951), 106-7.

Gloucestershire
Gloucester, Southgate Street; Atkin, *PMA*, 21 (1987), 1-24; Atkin, *Fortress*, 10 (1991), 32-8.

Hampshire
Basing House; Pike and Combley, *PHFCAS* (1964-6), 11-20; Moorhouse, *PMA*, 4 (1970), 31-91.

Hereford and Worcester
Worcester, Fort Royal; *PMA*, 4 (1970), 175.
Worcester, King's School; *PMA*, 1 (1967), 108.

North Yorkshire
Skipton, Park Hill; *YAJ* (1938).
York, Baile Hill; Addyman, *Arch J*, 134 (1977), 115-56.
York, Holgate Hill; Corder, *YAYAS* (1951-2), 31ff.
York, Lamel Hill; Thurnam, *Arch J*, 4 (1849), 27-39.

Nottinghamshire
Newark-on-Trent, Colonel Gray's Sconce; Manning, *TS*, 62 (1958), 36-42.
Newark-on-Trent, Millgate; Dean, *TS*, 72 (1968), 68-70.
Newark-on-Trent, Victoria Street; Drage, *TS*, 91 (1987), 127-32.
Nottingham Castle; Drage, *TS*, 93 (1989), 1-151.
Winthorpe, Redoubt 11B; Kinsley, *TS*, 92 (1988), 78.

Oxfordshire
Abingdon; *Current Archaeology*, 121 (1990), 27.
Wallingford Castle; *PMA*, 7 (1973), 100-17.

Shropshire
Shrewsbury, Roushill Wall; Brown and Watson, *Transactions of the Shropshire Archaeological Society*, 66 (1989), 85-9.

Somerset
Taunton; *PMA*, 12 (1978), 110.

Tyne and Wear
Newcastle upon Tyne, Black Gate; Ellison, Finch and Harbottle, *PMA*, 13 (1979), 153-81.
Newcastle upon Tyne, Castle; Ellison and Harbottle, *AA*, fifth series, 11 (1983), 135-263.
Newcastle upon Tyne, Orchard Street; *PMA*, 23 (1989), 47.

West Yorkshire
Pontefract Castle; West Yorkshire Archaeological Service, *Pontefract Castle* (1988).
Sandal Castle; Mayes and Butler (1983).

Wiltshire
Devizes; Haslam, *Wiltshire Archaeological Magazine*, 72/73 (1980), 59-65.

SCOTLAND
Dumfries and Galloway
Burnswark; Jobey, *TDGNHAS*, 50 (1973), 72-81.

Lothian
Edinburgh Castle; *PMA*, 24 (1990), 171.

WALES
Dyfed
Carew Castle; Gerrard, *Fortress*, 6 (1990), 45-50.
Carmarthen, Greyfriars; James, *CA*, 27 (1991), 21-30.

Mid Glamorgan
Caerphilly; Lewis, *Arch Camb*, 115 (1964-6), 67-87.

Powys
Montgomery Castle; *PMA*, 3 (1969).

10
Further reading

The following are recommended for further reading on the archaeology of the Civil War:

Allcroft, A. H. *Earthwork of England*. London, 1908.

Atkin, M. 'The Civil War Defences of Gloucester', *Fortress*, 10 (August 1991), 32-8.

Barley, M. W. 'The Queen's Sconce', *Transactions of the Thoroton Society*, 61 (1957), 27-32.

Besly, E. *English Civil War Coin Hoards*. British Museum, London, 1987.

Besly, E. 'A Civil War Hoard from Breckenborough, North Yorkshire', *Yorkshire Numismatist*, 1 (1988), 45-55.

Besly, E. *Coins and Medals of the English Civil War*. Seaby, London, 1990.

Bradley, R. 'Maumbury Rings, Dorchester: The Excavations of 1908-1913', *Archaeologia*, 105 (1975), 1-97.

Brown, T. M., and Watson, M. D. 'The Civil War Roushill Wall, Shrewsbury', *Transactions of the Shropshire Archaeological Society*, 66 (1989), 85-9.

Curphey, R. A. 'The Coastal Batteries 1. The Lord's Defences to the Revetment', *Journal of the Manx Museum*, 7 (1967), 50-7.

Curphey, R. A. 'The Fort at Bishopscourt, Isle of Man', *Post-Medieval Archaeology*, 8 (1974), 104-7.

Dean, M. J. 'Civil War Siege Defences, Millgate, Newark', *Transactions of the Thoroton Society*, 72 (1968), 68-70.

Drage, C. 'An Excavation of the Royalist Town Ditch at Victoria Street, Newark, Nottinghamshire, 1986', *Transactions of the Thoroton Society*, 91 (1987), 127-32.

Ellison, M., Finch, M., and Harbottle, B. 'The Excavation of a 17th Century Pit at the Black Gate, Newcastle-upon-Tyne, 1975', *Post-Medieval Archaeology*, 13 (1979), 153-81.

Ellison, M., and Harbottle, B. 'The Excavation of a 17th-Century Bastion in the Castle of Newcastle upon Tyne, 1976-81', *Archaeologia Aeliana*, fifth series, 11 (1983), 135-263.

Gaunt, P. *The Cromwellian Gazetteer*. Alan Sutton, Gloucester, 1987.

Gaunt, P. *A Nation under Siege: the Civil War in Wales*. HMSO, London, for CADW Wales, 1991.

Harrington, P. 'English Civil War Fortifications', *Fort*, 15 (1987), 39-59.

James, T. A. 'Carmarthen's Civil War Defences: Discoveries at Carmarthen Greyfriars Excavations 1983-1990', *Carmarthenshire Antiquary*, 27 (1991), 21-30.

Jobey, G. 'A Military Redoubt on Burnswark Hill, Dumfriesshire', *Transactions of the Dumfriesshire and Galloway Natural History and Antiquarian Society*, 50 (1973), 72-81.

Kent, P. *Fortifications of East Anglia*. Terence Dalton, Lavenham, 1988.

Kenyon, J. R. 'The Civil War Earthworks around Raglan Castle, Gwent: an Aerial View', *Archaeologia Cambrensis*, 131 (1982), 139-42.

Kenyon, J. R. 'A Cannon Shot Mould from Raglan Castle', *Archaeologia Cambrensis*, 131 (1982), 142-4.

Kenyon, J. R. *Raglan Castle*. CADW: Welsh Historic Monuments, 1988.

Kerrigan, P. M. 'Seventeenth Century Fortifications, Forts and Garrisons in Ireland: a Preliminary List', *The Irish Sword*, 14 (1980), 3-24, 135-56.

Keynes, G. L., and White, H. G. 'Excavations at Earith Bulwark', *Proceedings of the Cambridgeshire Antiquarian Society*, 50 (1908), 157-261.

Kinsley, G. 'Excavation on the Supposed Site of Civil War Redoubt 11B, Newark-on-Trent, Nottinghamshire', *Transactions of the Thoroton Society*, 92 (1988), 78.

Lewis, J. M. 'The Roman Fort and Civil War Earthworks at Caerphilly', *Archaeologia Cambrensis*, 115 (1964-6), 67-87.

Manchester, K. 'Palaeopathology of a Royalist Garrison', *OSSA: Journal of the Osteological Laboratory*, 5 (1979), 25-33.

Manning, W. H. 'Excavations at Colonel Gray's Sconce, near Newark, in July, 1958', *Thoroton Society Transactions*, 62 (1958), 36-42.

Mayes, P., and Butler, L. *Sandal Castle Excavations 1964-1973. A Detailed Archaeological Report*. Wakefield Historical Publications, Wakefield, 1983.

Mayhew, N., and Viner, C. 'A Civil War Coin Hoard from Weston-sub-Edge, Gloucestershire', *Transactions of the Bristol and Gloucestershire Archaeological Society*, 105 (1987), 213-22.

Newman, P. *The Battle of Marston Moor*. Anthony Bird Productions, Chichester, 1981.

O'Neil, B. H. St John. 'Dartmouth Castle and the Other Defences of Dartmouth Haven', *Archaeologia*, 85 (1936), 129ff.

O'Neil, B. H. St John. 'The Bulwarks, Carmarthen', *Archaeologia Cambrensis*, 93 (1938), 126-30.

O'Neil, B. H. St John. 'A Civil War Battery at Cornbury, Oxfordshire', *Oxoniensia*, 10 (1945), 73-8.

O'Neil, B. H. St John. *Castles and Cannon*. Oxford University Press, 1960.

O'Neil, B. H. St John. *Ancient Monuments of the Isles of Scilly*. HMSO, London, 1961.

Osborne, M. *Cromwellian Fortifications in Cambridgeshire*. Cromwell Museum, Huntingdon, 1990.

Pontefract Castle. The Archaeology of the Civil War. West Yorkshire Archaeological Service, Wakefield, 1988.

Ratcliffe, J., and Sharpe, A. 'Practical Management Work at Oliver's Battery, Tresco', in *Fieldwork in Scilly, Autumn, 1990*, Cornwall Archaeological Unit, Truro, 1990.

Ross, W. E. 'Military Engineering during the Great Civil War', *Professional Papers of the Corps of Royal Engineers*, 1887 (reprinted 1984).

RCHM. *Newark on Trent. The Civil War Siegeworks*. HMSO, London, 1964.

RCHM. *York, Volume 2: The Defences*. HMSO, London, 1972.

RCHM. *Change and Continuity*. HMSO, London, 1991.

Saunders, A. D. 'Earith Bulwark', *Archaeological Journal*, 124 (1967), 222-3.

Stoyle, M. *Exeter City Defences Project. Documentary Evidence of the Civil War Defences of Exeter, 1642-3*. Exeter Museums Archaeological Field Unit, Exeter, 1988.

Stoyle, M. *The Civil War Defences of Exeter and the Great Parliamentary Siege of 1645-46*. Exeter Museums Archaeological Field Unit Report Number 90.26, Exeter, 1990.

Taylor, C. *Fieldwork in Medieval Archaeology*. Batsford, London, 1974.

Ward, S. *Excavations at Chester. The Civil War Siegeworks 1642-6*. Grosvenor Museum Archaeological Excavation and Survey Reports Number 4, Chester, 1987.

Woolrych, A. *Battles of the English Civil War*. Batsford, London, 1961.

Young, P. *Edgehill 1642. The Campaign and the Battle*. The Roundwood Press, Kineton, 1967.

Index

Page numbers in italics refer to illustrations.